DC ANE

Personal stories of life on the Isle of Wight before 1970

Edited by
Helen Butler BSc
for

INDEPENDENT ARTS

Charity No:297474 Company limited by guarantee No: 2147908

First published by
Red Squirrel Enterprises 2009
Printed by Crossprint Ltd
ISBN No: 978-0-9552314-4-5

Acknowledgements

Besley
Steve Lambert
Barry Price
Wendy Varley
Red Squirrel Enterprises
The authors who took the time and trouble to record their stories for posterity

SPONSORS:

Contents

Introduction: Independent Arts Story by Helen Butler	6
Ryde Pier - A poem by Ray Wesley Jones	8
My Life as an Isle of Wight Nipper by Malcolm Groves	9
Wolf Cubs and Boy Scouts by Malcolm Groves	12
Newport not so long ago by Ted Denness	14
Newport Market in the 1920's by David Martin	17
A Newport Medical Practice by Dr Paul Hooper	19
My Stories by Dinah Boulter:	
Starting School	23
Discipline at School	26
Dinner Money	27
Physical Education Lessons	28
Learning to use the Telephone	29
My First Shop Permanent Wave	32
The Dentist	34
My Life and Career after the War by Bill Madden	36
Life at Chale School 1947-1953 by Derek Sprake	41
Post War Ryde by Sandie Owens	50
Life in Shorwell during the War by Peggy Thomson	53
Life in the Women's Land Army by Sybil Groves	60
Memories of Freshwater Fruit Farm by John Craddock	63
Reflections on Farming prior to 1970 by Malcolm Dyer	68
My Life in the Wilderness by Alan Philpott	70

INTRODUCTION

INDEPENDENT ARTS STORY by Helen Butler

It may seem strange for a charity with the title 'Independent Arts' to be producing a memories book but reminiscence is actually a popular part of the charity's work as it can be used to stimulate art or craft work or simply as a group session for older people in residential homes. It is during these sessions that fascinating stories emerge and this is how the idea for the book was formed.

Although the authors are not from residential homes, most wrote the stories themselves and generally only minimal editing was required. The Isle of Wight way of speaking is left in just as the authors wrote it.

Before the charity was registered as Independent Arts in 1987, it ran under the name of 'Blow Your Own Trumpet' and catered for people who had suffered a stroke, a Mr Parkes being the initial inspiration. In the early days, sessions included drama and poetry as well as the art-based and music sessions we still run. Independent Arts used to take these sessions into the prisons as well as the hospital, day centres and residential homes. We no longer go to the prisons but have added community projects for all special needs groups to our work.

Whilst sorting through old files, I found paperwork that showed there was a good membership of Island notables such as Anthony Minghella and his parents Gloria and Edward Minghella. Sheila Hancock was also an honorary member. Sadly, membership lapsed in the mid 1990's but we are currently bringing back corporate sponsorship and 'Friends of Independent Arts' (see last page) as Independent Arts can offer members some exciting events and involvement in community projects. We are delighted Alan Titchmarsh has agreed to become an honorary patron.

From humble beginnings (the charity was first run from the director's front room), Independent Arts has grown into an organisation that helps hundreds of people with special needs and older people on the Isle of Wight.

We were the first to introduce Soundbeam ('an invisible, expanding keyboard in space') to the Island which has benefitted many severely disabled people as well as other groups and school children. We look forward to extending services and community projects and helping many more people take part in the arts - and most of all to have fun - in the years to come.

I hope you enjoy reading these stories and gain an insight into life on the Isle of Wight in the early and mid part of the 20th century. As Ryde is often referred to as 'The Gateway to the Island', the first contribution is a poem about Ryde Pier.

RYDE PIER
A poem by Ray Wesley Jones

Nostalgic thoughts of gleaming track
From Cowes and Ventnor, there and back
Carefree childhood days, when those rails fed
Passengers to Ryde Pier Head.

Life seemed filled with sunlit days
As we went about our lawful ways
At Island schools, which sometimes led
To mainland trips from Ryde Pier Head.

The pier leans out across the sands,
Welcoming with open hands;
It stands proudly, boats beside
Bobbing and bouncing on the tide.

It beckons now as it did then
So many years ago. Remember when
The paddles churned and steam trains fled
Between the shore and Ryde Pier Head.

Imagine our young delight
Belonging to the Isle of Wight.
Pompey wins at Fratton Park,
Sailing home into the dark.

Young hearts beating, we were sure
We'd live there for evermore.
I was wrong but happy 'cos
I remember Ryde Pier as it was.

MY LIFE AS AN ISLE OF WIGHT NIPPER
by Malcolm Groves

Whitepit Lane is a busy thoroughfare nowadays but back in 1954 we kids used it as a playground. Cars were scarcely seen and traffic was mostly limited to the daily milk float, lemonade lorry, dust cart or the occasional steamroller, which caused great excitement.

If you wanted your daily pinta, it was a matter of taking a jug to the milk float and getting it filled from a churn. There were no fridges so the milk jug was kept on a marble slab and covered in muslin.

The dust cart wasn't the relatively sophisticated piece of machinery it is today but merely a lorry with sliding lids that were lifted manually and the dustbin lifted and tipped in.

The lemonade lorry would come round much as an ice cream van does today. Soft drinks played their part in my first job, which was for Gould Hibberd and Randall. This business was situated at Church Litten and a plaque survives on the wall today marking its former presence in the town. I worked packing the soft drink 'Hubbly Bubbly' into crates for all of one week and then moved onto crisps, as Gould Hibberd and Randall had the franchise for the only brand of crisps available at the time - Smiths.

In 1962 Smiths crisps could only be bought in a pub, not in the shops. They came with a twist of salt and cost 4d which is less than 2p in today's money. Crisps didn't keep as well in those days - I guess preservatives were either not used or not as effective as they are now. The packaging certainly wasn't, as there weren't the plastics, only treated paper. I enjoyed delivering crisps as it was easy to carry 10 boxes which looked good and impressed the young ladies! Supermarkets have replaced the small

specialised shops we had in the 1960s. I remember a grocers shop called Attrills in Carisbrooke that had a wall of little drawers and a big wooden counter. You could buy any quantity of food and it was wrapped up in paper. If it was sugar you were buying, for instance, it was weighed to whatever you wanted and put into a cone of paper. Bacon was ordered by a number that related to the thickness of the bacon you wanted and the machine sliced off however many slices you needed - there was no pre-packaging in those days!

In the early 1960s, I joined the 69 club. Quite why it was called the 69 club, I don't know. Technology didn't feature much in the equipment used and faithful roadies would struggle to keep the show going. One Saturday night at the 69 Club, The Move was playing when staging and equipment collapsed during the performance! Being true troupers, the band crawled from under the wreckage and kept going as the roadies soldered everything back together again! Health and Safety would have a fit nowadays!

Even big names such The Rolling Stones would come to the Island as groups toured and didn't mind playing to small groups of people. Everyone could afford to go, as ticket prices were reasonable. The local group was The Cherokees and they covered all the popular hits and I recall they were excellent.

The Babalu Club, the first disco on the Island, was 'posh' and had table service and basket meals. As it was situated out in the country (by Ryde Airport - where Tesco is now) it was hard to get there unless you had a lift. Because it was 'off the beaten track' it was not unusual to come out at 2am and walk home to Newport!

Another source of entertainment was at the Seagull Ballroom at the end of Ryde Pier. There wasn't a car park at the end of the pier but there were amusement machines and the one I particularly remember used to punch your name out on a metal strip. Of course the pier was very different then as there were actually three piers - one for the train, one for cars and one with a tramline for a shuttle service up and down the pier.

Travelling by ferry was a different experience as well. There were no fastcats - just a slow boat that in the summer would be crammed with factory employees on their annual

holiday together. Mainland coaches didn't come over as they do now and the car ferry was very much smaller, so Southern Vectis, Moss Motors and Fountain Coaches had the job of transporting the holidaymakers to the camps. If there was a long queue on the pier - as often happened - then entertainers from the holiday camps would come along to keep spirits up.

The winters seemed colder - no central heating or fleeces then. The summers were warmer - do I really remember standing in a shelter at Ryde to keep out of the rain? We tried to do less - no cars to rush around in. We were less well off - sweets were still on ration too. Were we happier? We probably were.

WOLF CUBS AND BOY SCOUTS by Malcolm Groves

Well that's what they were called when I was a lad. If you gained enough badges in the Wolf Cubs, you could achieve your Leaping Wolf badge and wear it proudly on your Boy Scout uniform. I remember in addition to a range of tests to achieve my stars, I had to complete my First Aider Proficiency Badge.

Gaining badges wasn't what it was mainly about for most of us. I enjoyed thundering up and down the upstairs hall at Carisbrooke Sunday School playing boisterous games like British Bulldog.

Malcolm Groves (second left) and friends 1963

When I joined the Boy Scouts, I transferred to 6th Newport as they met on the one night of the week that I didn't have to do any homework. It was great fun. We were bigger lads tearing around burning off a lot of energy as well as learning a lot.

I don't want to give the impression we were hooligans but we seemed to have an abundance of energy to burn off. We did all sorts of things, mainly in the scout hall in the winter and out and about in the summer. I also recall regular Sunday church parades at St John's.

My favourite activity was camping in the summer at

Corf Camp near Shalfleet. Back then there was virtually nothing there except the land and it was fairly overgrown. We used to load up a trek cart in Newport on a Friday evening with an old army surplus bell tent and enough food for the weekend. We tied the whole lot on with rope and then with two pulling the cart's centre shaft and the rest pulling on ropes attached to the side, off we ran.

Seems hard to believe but back then there was no problem running along the road with a trek cart. There was virtually no traffic at that time of the day and not much at any time. On one notable occasion, I recall we managed to turn the whole kit and caboodle over going round a corner and I ended up in the bottom of a ditch out Porchfield way with the lot on top of me and surrounded by broken biscuits. We were a bit short on food that weekend!

Food was a strange mixture. Baked beans on toast played a prominent role along with Instant Whip (just add cold milk and try to stir out the lumps). We also used to cook a lot of stews. I guess it was because we only needed one large pan and when thickened up with a couple of handfuls of porridge oats it was very filling.

The big advantage of Corf was that we could swim in the creek. If the weather was fine and the tide was right, we could have a good old mud battle and then clean up when the sea came in. We also had special salt-water soap although it never seemed to achieve much in the way of lather.

I look back now with great fondness on my time as a Boy Scout. At the time, it just seemed like fun with my mates. How little did I understand the range of skills that I was acquiring and how, without being lectured, I was able to learn about teamwork and leadership. All of it was managed without the benefit of risk assessments and paperwork. Was that unwise? At that time, I think not.

NEWPORT NOT SO LONG AGO by Ted Denness

The main change that strikes me nowadays is the number of small shops and businesses that have gone. When I got married, we lived in a small cottage in Nodehill and in those days, fifty-odd years ago, Upper St James was busy with small shops. Besides Ralph's, there were two greengrocers to choose from, Mr Best and Mrs West; two sweet shops, Mrs Bannister and Mr Payne; five pubs, from the Cranbourne down to the George, with the Plough, The Grapes and one other between; a grocers (Cave & Sherwood), a butcher (Mr Gustar) and a pork-butcher (Mr Kirby): an outfitters (Whitcher), a cleaners (Bright & Minns) and a handbag shop (Wavell), along with a Post Office (Mr Rook), Snellgroves the decorators, Barnes the barber, Shutler's bakery and a good few more besides. There was everything along Nodehill, from Margarets (children's clothing) to Mr Cooper the stonemason - all there in Upper St James, no need ever to go further for anything.

Gustars circa 1960

The buildings haven't altered greatly, but not too many of the businesses have survived. Before it was Margaret's for kiddies' clothes, that shop belonged to Mr Coward the oil man. He dealt with paraffin and similar and that was where we went for candles. Our house didn't have electricity when we moved in. There was a gas cooker (and one gas light), though supplies failed in harsh winters like 1953.

We did eventually get electricity put in - one light upstairs and one down. Each week the coalman delivered for the fire - that man's horse knew exactly where to stop each time. I reckon that horse knew the round better than anyone!

It was the same story with shops in the rest of town. The High Street, from Wrays at the top down to the ice-cream factory at the bottom, was packed out with local businesses - butchers (Trevor Reynolds), fishmonger (Cole), pork-butcher (Lower), ironmongers (Tyler's), chemist (Pollard & Ramage) and so on. In those days shops stayed in the family, handed down for the next generation to take over, and I think they gave better service than nowadays. Though I remember one shop-owner telling her assistant, 'If a customer comes in, don't let them go out without buying something.'

I was born in Castle Road. My father was foreman miller at Ford Mill, which was beyond Mr Guy the wheelwrights at the bottom of Pyle Street. The mill was shut down and demolished when they built the big roundabout there [1962]. There were several mills working along the Medina in the Thirties. Ford milled flour and different types of animal feed, cattle cake, nuts and such like, which then got delivered out to the farms by lorry. One of my early memories is of watching a man chisel out the grooves on a millstone in the traditional pattern. I also remember my father saying at times of heavy rain that he'd have to get down to the mill to

raise the floodgates.

When it came to my turn to start earning, my father sent me down to Southern Vectis to see if I could get a job there. I must have walked in at just the right time, as they said, 'Right, you start next week' and I think it was five bob [25p today] a week that I started on. The apprenticeship took seven years. First you spent a year washing off and cleaning up engine parts. Then you had a year in the stores to get to know all the parts, then a year in welding, a year with the electricians and so on. I don't know that I'd have chosen that job if I'd had the choice - but you didn't get much choice in those days. Given half a chance, I guess I'd have preferred farming.

I used to help out on a farm on Saturdays as a small boy, aged seven or so. The farmer would give me a lift out to the farm, saying, 'I'll be round for you half-past seven in the morning, Nipper' - and I wouldn't get back till eight at night. It was tiring, feeding the horses and similar jobs, and I got paid in pastry - a triangular apple puff. I enjoyed it in the summer but it was cold in winter. My parents couldn't afford good clothes, so when it snowed, you froze. Good old days? Cold old days, anyway!

NEWPORT MARKET IN THE 1920'S
by David Martin

In the 1920s, when I was a schoolboy, one of my pleasures was to visit Newport market, which in those days was in St James' Square. The cattle market was on a Tuesday, but on Saturdays the 'cheapjacks' came over from Portsmouth to sell their wares to the unsophisticated 'caulkheads' of the island who were up in town looking for a bargain.

I was especially interested in one man, who was selling watch chains. When a small crowd had gathered, he held up a chain for all to see, saying that although it was not gold, it was made of a metal that looked like gold and wore like gold and was 'dug up in the bowels of California'. I can still remember him using that phrase today. They were a bargain, at half-a-crown each and, as an incentive, he would give to each buyer two small packets of free gifts, which he had wrapped up so that you couldn't see what they contained.

As a further encouragement, he took half a dozen watches and allowed the spectators to examine their quality. Then he wrapped them up as he had with the free gifts and muddled them all up.

Customers would then begin to buy, but as you have perhaps guessed, no packet with a watch appeared. When the buying stopped, the man held up a chain with two packets and shouted out 'Is there a buyer?'. With that he quickly opened one of the packets to reveal a watch, saying 'There's a watch you missed'. This would encourage a few more customers for a while. Only once, when he had a good crowd, did I ever see a watch won, and then he made a loud call, 'There's another watch won'.

One Saturday, when all the cheapjacks had gone, I was walking past his site and I saw one of his chains in the gutter. I picked it up and put it in my pocket. A week or two later, on taking it out, I found I only had an iron chain. The coating on it had worn off, in that short time, in my pocket. I often wonder if today anyone would get away with this way of selling.

A NEWPORT MEDICAL PRACTICE
by Dr Paul Hooper

Dr Hooper circa 1987

I remember my father telling me that that in the early part of the 19th century, if the doctor was called out in the night to see a patient in Rookley, for example, a boy would cycle in with the message. The ostler would then harness the pony and trap and while the doctor drove out to see his patient, the boy would sleep in the hayloft. On his return the doctor would make up his prescription and the boy would cycle back to the patient with it!

The doctor's practice was located in the house of Dr Stanley Foster, as it had been in the days of his father. It was situated at the lower end of the High Street on the site of the present Police Station and the garden, which boasted a tennis court, extended south to reach Pyle Street where the coach-house lay.

At about this time, Dr Foster was joined by Dr Coombes. He was born in St Nicholas House in the High Street, where Woolworths used to be, but at this time he built a house on the corner of Whitepit Lane and St Johns Road. He named it St Nicholas House as it still is now. He did not enjoy good health and retired just before or during the first World War. His daughter, Josephine, worked for the Seely

Estate at Brook and retired to a house in Cypress Road, when she became my patient. I remember her as a very gracious lady.

At the end of the war, Dr Foster was joined by Dr Jack Dowdall. He was an Irishman from Dublin and had done part of his training at the famous Rotunda Maternity Hospital. His expertise in obstetrics resulted in his being called out to places all over the island to help with difficult births. He saw patients in the conservatory of the house in the lower High Street, sometimes with the rain dripping on him (or his patient) from the leaky roof. Morning surgery would begin at 9.30am but before that, he had often done a sick parade in Parkhurst Prison and played a game of squash on the court there. Presumably Dr Foster saw his patients in his own consulting room, which was attached to the dispensary. At this time, Florrie Johnson joined the practice as a trainee dispenser and was a much loved fixture until she retired in the 1970's, by which time she was known as Dr Johnson!

Surgeries took place morning and evening on six days a week (including Saturday evening) and ten patients a session would be considered very busy. It sometimes happened that at an evening surgery Jack would turn up in his dinner jacket, so the patient would say 'Oh I see you are going out so I won't keep you long'. Actually Jack was probably going up to the County Club to play bridge!

After morning surgery there would be visits, which were common in the days of limited public transport. I recall Dr Foster was one of the first people on the island to own a motor car. So things went on pleasantly until the Second World War came in 1939 and some Island doctors were called up to the services and their places were taken by those remaining. Dr Foster and Dr Dowdall took on the area around Shorwell and Brighstone, with the result that many years later the practice still had patients in the area.

Just after the war Dr Foster retired and shortly after died, so the house at the lower end of the High Street had to be vacated, but Dr Dowdall was able to rent the Dower House in Pyle Street where the practice still resides, although in much altered premises. Why the 'Dower' House? No one really knows - the 'Dower' to what? Was there a manor at Newport? Certainly it is a Tudor building, for when alterations were made, a Tudor fireplace was uncovered. Mr Macket, the stonemason at Balls the building firm, was certain the stone came from the ruins of Quarr Abbey. The house is just a few paces from the old Chantry House.

The Dower House

Shortly before the advent of the National Health Service in 1948, Dr Dowdall was joined by Dr Richard Sandiford. The health service resulted in many changes - surgeries became much busier, as did the demands for home visits and, with Dr Dowdall ageing, an enormous workload fell on the shoulders of Dr Sandiford. With the impending retirement of Dr Dowdall in 1960, I joined the practice in the autumn of 1959, and this was followed by a period of expansion by amalgamation with other practices. In 1961

Dr Terry brought his patients to the Dower House on the retirement of his partner, Dr Peskett. In 1967 Dr Orr joined, on the retirement of his partner, Dr Dennis McCann. By this time the practice list had risen to about 13,000 patients or about one tenth of the then island population. Hospital appointments soon followed. Dr Sandiford worked in the Psychiatric Dept, Drs Terry and Orr were attached to the newly built Maternity Unit at St Marys Hospital, and Dr Hooper joined the Surgical Dept, so there was plenty to do. Radio telephones were fitted in the cars and rotas fixed to cover out-of-hours work. Moreover, some small research projects were undertaken and some papers published. Minor surgery and developmental baby clinics were also established.

It was during this period that the Royal College of General Practitioners was becoming more influential and all the partners were members of it. Dr Sandiford was increasingly asked to visit and advise practices across the Island and in the Wessex area on the mainland which involved his being away at times, so it was decided to appoint a fourth partner and Dr Mobbs joined in 1975. Then in 1977 Dr Orr left to work abroad and was replaced by Dr Robert Kumar. With increasing ages, the hospital appointments were gradually relinquished. Dr Sandiford retired in 1982 and then Drs Hooper and Terry in the 1990's, by which time there were two female partners, Drs Maureen Simmonds and Hester Clarke - all somewhat different to 1900!

MY STORIES by Dinah Boulter

STARTING SCHOOL

Dinah Boulter circa 1949

As I lived in a small rural village and my father had opted for me to go to Godshill Primary School, some three miles or more from Whitwell, the only way to get there in time for the start of the school day was by steam train. A long walk to the station (for four year old legs) and a journey in the old slam-door carriages for about twenty minutes and I arrived at Godshill station. My brother travelled on to the Grammar School at Newport and probably pushed me out at the stop until I could remember to get myself out.

After arriving at Godshill, I trudged up the long lane that connected the station to the main road. I was to meet up with two girls who lived in the thatched cottage on the corner.

Joan was the older and Margaret the younger, and they lived there with their mum and dad. They always seemed to be late, trying to slurp at over filled cups of tea whilst their mother brushed their hair in haste. If they didn't stand still, mum served a swift clump with the back of a large flat-backed hairbrush on their bottoms. Mum usually won the struggle and both had large amounts of hair securely tied up with even bigger white bows of ribbon. We were all ready for school. Joan was in charge, as she was the oldest, and we were marched down a busy road to the local primary school.

There were those who lived in quite remote areas, on farms, in the outlying districts and these souls had to walk to school, rain or shine. They all managed to turn up though, boys in short grey trousers with a 'v' necked sleeveless pullover and the girls in a navy skirt or gymslip with a yellow sash and blue cardigan. The one thing I loved wearing most was the gold and navy tie, although most of the time I guess this looked like a straggly length of string tied around my neck, making my shirt collar appear to take off! My father nicknamed me 'Collar Kingswell' at a very early age.

Most of the children turned up each day in clean enough uniforms although some were late to school or absent altogether because they had been helping with the lambing or harvesting. I envied these children as I never had an excuse to miss a days schooling. My father was the school attendance and welfare officer, easily recognised in his 'Trilby' hat, tweed suit, pipe and a bone conducting hearing aid. Even today some boys remember him - usually the naughty ones!

On the first day of school I can remember being awarded a black mark in prayers and being made to stand at the front of the whole school assembly with other naughty children to admit my crime. Miss Moody, the headmistress, dressed in a black academic gown and mortar board, awarded the mark and I can still feel the deep embarrassment sixty years on.

These were the days of gas lights in the school room, hard wooden desks, 'flight commander' pen nibs and very wet, very black ink and an inkwell set into the top of the desk. Many things I could not do - but I was very good at smudging my work!

On my father's frequent visits to the school when he checked the registers to see who was absent and find out why, I was often asked to 'come up the front Dinah and show your father your books'. I dreaded these visits as, although the first page of a new book was often neat and tidy, smudges ensued in much of the rest of the book - they were a mess! How unfair I felt this was, as no one else's parent came to the school so often. Little did I know at that stage in my life how many times similar embarrassments would occur over the next twelve years!

DISCIPLINE AT SCHOOL by Dinah Boulter

When PC Thatcher called at the school, we knew that we were going to get a lecture about how to behave and the sort of things that children were and were not expected to do. Tall in his stockinged feet, dressed in his full uniform with very large shiny black boots and pointed helmet, he looked like a scary giant to us small beings. Two of his sons attended the school and, unlike these days, I don't remember them being bullied or picked on because of their dad's job.

No doubt there was an element of 'naughtiness' in the village and outlying districts but I never heard of anyone flouting the law to any great degree, although one or two of the boys were troublesome. The headmaster kept a long, bendy cane in the corner of his room for all to see and this was used on a few occasions but not before other punishment had failed to bring the child into line. I can remember one boy was eventually caned after continuously behaving badly. After the first stroke of the withy cane, he snatched it from the master's hand, broke it in half and ran home. I imagine that PC Thatcher and my father were involved in his punishment. I understand that the boy and his brother both eventually became eminent doctors in some part of the country.

Discipline ruled everywhere and anyone stepping out of line, if they were not punished at school, had the wrath of their parents to contend with when they got home, either by mother wielding a wooden spoon or stick kept for the purpose, or by father with his belt - and it didn't do us any harm!

DINNER MONEY by Dinah Boulter

Taking the school dinner money to the Post Office could only be done when we were considered by the teacher to be responsible enough to be entrusted with this task.

In those days there were 240 pennies in the pound (480 half pennies or 960 farthings) and the pound was a note. There were also three penny bits, silver sixpences, florins, 10 shilling notes and five pound notes (large and white). It always fascinated me how the Postmaster could count the coins so quickly and arrange them in neat piles of the same denomination.

The silver sixpences and three penny bits were especially prized as these could be put into the Christmas pudding and, if you were lucky, you got the coin on Christmas Day. You had to be careful of course when eating the pudding in case you swallowed the coin or crunched down with your teeth onto it, making a trip to the dentist necessary! The silver sixpenny was sometimes placed beneath a pillow to replace a saved tooth and then we knew that the tooth fairy had visited during the night.

PHYSICAL EDUCATION LESSONS
by Dinah Boulter

A rather stern lady, called Miss Privet, came to teach P.E. on one or two days of the week. I guess this was to teach us skills in dexterity and hand and eye co-ordination. We all thought she must have been in the forces as a physical training instructor because all exercises and games were carried out by numbers. The boys wore navy shorts or the short grey uniform trousers and singlet, whilst the girls wore vest and knickers.

The lessons were all carried out on the asphalt playground and if anyone had a fall that was just hard luck. Grazed knees and elbows were commonplace. No fuss was made, few plasters given, no school nurse or rest room. We were just expected to get up and carry on - and accident books had not been thought of. The odd one or two may have suffered broken limbs at some time but I do not remember any occasion when any fuss was made because a child had been asked to do an exercise which had resulted in hospitalisation.

Any floor exercises involved were done on a thin mat. Bean bags were useful items for throwing and aiming, I guess because there was little damage that one could inflict with these, as they were filled with real dried peas or beans.

No one would dare to eat any fillings for fear of retribution if caught.

I can remember landing on my elbow whilst practising the high jump over a cane balanced between two uprights. Only a very thin, hard mat broke my fall and I must have injured something because I had to see the doctor and he wrapped the whole of my torso in thick adhesive plaster. I had to keep this in place for about a month, by which time it was a little smelly, grubby and very irritating.

My mother bought a pot of solvent from the chemist which was supposed to 'melt' the stickiness of the plaster enabling it to be peeled off easily. No such luck! Inch by inch we worked away at the offending stuff until the last nine inches were left and, in desperation, my mother peeled a corner back, distracted me by some means and ripped the rest of the plaster off in one go. I was so relieved to feel the freedom of a soft vest on my skin at last that I forgave my mother. 'I had to be a little cruel to be kind Dinah', she said.

LEARNING TO USE THE TELEPHONE
by Dinah Boulter

Not many homes had telephones in the 1950s and, although we had one in our house at Whitwell, it was treated as something almost supernatural and most people were afraid to use it.

The phone at home was installed to assist my father in his day to day job. Any calls had to be logged into a carefully ruled up book (this done by my father in a most meticulous way) and the length of time spent on the call as well as the number called had to be written in correctly. Any

members of the family using the phone for seemingly trivial reasons were duly remonstrated with.

The first telephone I can remember in the home was a 'stick' one made from black Bakelite. This had a dial in the base and a small tube connected to the appliance by the wire which was held to the ear. The small funnel shaped orifice was for speaking into. In time this contraption was replaced by a new phone - still Bakelite but the ear and mouth piece were combined into a hand-held arrangement, one end to be placed next to the ear, the other to be spoken into. When not in use this was rested onto a 'cradle' thus cutting off the connecting line. There was a dial with numbers from 0 to 9 set out around a circle of metal which, when dialled, returned to its placed with a ratcheting sound.

Although an official red telephone box stood outside the Post Office, in times of stress, our neighbours would knock on the door and ask to use our phone - much to my father's annoyance. They would ask for him to do the dialling and get through to the caller, more often than not the doctor.

Perhaps it was because of a general fear of using the telephone that two children at a time were sent to the local telephone box just along the road from the school to practice using the instrument.

With the heavy old coins jangling in our pockets, we were told to lift off the receiver and listen for the dialling tone, then place the pennies in the slot and wait for these to drop into the box. We then had to dial the school number and let it ring three times, although it would not be answered. The next trick was to press button 'B' and the coins put in to make the call would come tumbling out of the box into a small chute. These had to be taken out and returned to the school.

On rare occasions, when we were deemed competent enough to make a call, button 'A' was to be pressed, thus connecting the caller with the teacher at the other end. On even rarer occasions, we were allowed to call the emergency service, by dialling '999' but this could only be done because there was a local exchange near to the telephone box and the school teachers had arranged for it to happen, without any of the services rushing out to assist us! A very useful lesson.

MY FIRST SHOP PERMANENT WAVE
by Dinah Boulter

It must have been about 1957, when I was fourteen or fifteen, that I was allowed to go to a hairdresser's salon, Bretts in Spring Hill, Ventnor, to have my first professional permanent wave.

I had enjoyed the benefits of home perms on several occasions before this event. Advertisements in ladies' magazines made us ask 'Does one have the 'Toni' or 'Twink' - these being the names given to the lotions used to make straight hair curl. Using either of these products involved making sure that my father was busy in another room or at a meeting as the awful smell of ammonia from the perm lotion penetrated the whole house for some time.

To use the product, the hair had to be sectioned off methodically and each segment sponged with the cold lotion, wrapped in a tough tissue paper length and rolled up to the scalp around pink and blue plastic curlers. These had to be tight or they would fall out. More lotion was then sponged on each curler, the head wrapped loosely, turban-style, in a towel and left for about twenty minutes or so depending on the tightness of curl required. A sausage of cotton wool was pushed around the hair line, underneath each curler, to stop the lotion running down my neck, but most of the time this wasn't very successful and I remember the feel of the cold lotion dripping down my neck.

After the allotted time, copious amounts of water were poured over the head at the scullery sink with jugs and a bowl of warm water. We didn't have a shower and we were certainly not allowed to go to the bathroom in case father needed the toilet.

The curlers were then 'blotted' with yet another towel

and the cold neutraliser squeezed along each curler. Another ten or twenty minutes later, when I was wet all down my back, everything had to be well washed off again and the plastic curlers taken out.

We then set the hair onto large rollers, covered everything with a pink or blue hairnet and hoped that the heavy, hand-held metal drier would work. Eventually, after what seemed like a very long time, the moment of truth came and the rollers were taken out and my hair brushed carefully into place. My hair was usually very curly and looked like a frizzy mop but I knew that eventually it would be nice to look at.

Going to the hairdressers for a perm was a bit different. I guess the same preparations took place with the lotions, but the hair was rolled onto special rollers, attached to electrical elements of some kind, and then plugged into a cable. I was placed beneath a hood of some kind and my head felt very heavy. The bonus of the shop process was that there was a professional stylist to brush out and persuade my hair into place!

THE DENTIST by Dinah Boulter

We waited alone, one at a time in an empty classroom, until called to climb into the dentist's chair. Eventually my turn came.

Forget today's modern leather upholstered chair with padded arms and slick looking apparatus to be used in ones mouth. This was an ancient metal seat which may have had arm rests but I did not take much notice of these as my attention was focused on the overhead contraption that dangled down by my right side. The 'contraption' was a drill which was worked by a foot pedal driven by the dentist's leg - not always a smooth operation!

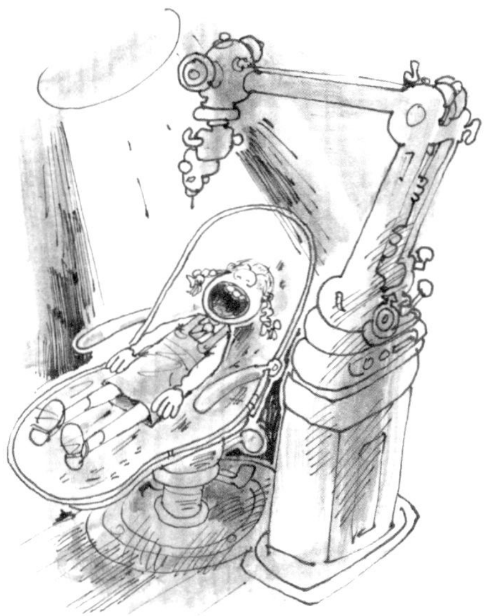

There were no injections to deaden the area to be treated. Copious wedges of cotton wool were pushed into my mouth to keep my cheek from getting in the way and push my tongue clear of the site to be worked on, keeping it dry and free from saliva. After an interminable and excruciating time with the drill, a long blast of cold dry air was pumped onto the site of the filling - this being even more painful. Then a metal plunger, filled with the mercury-based filling, was placed on the tooth and the contents rammed into the prepared cavity. That was it.

No nice nurse to hold a young child's hand, no happy face sticker for being a good little girl, and no mother to comfort me as she lived in Whitwell- three miles from the school- and it was difficult to get to Godshill on the bus.
I had made no fuss, I guess because I was brought up not to make a fuss so I didn't. Not even a gasp or groan as the screaming drill hit the nerve. That was my first experience with a dentist - I have had many more since!

MY LIFE AND CAREER ON THE ISLE OF WIGHT AFTER THE WAR by Bill Maden

Bill Madden 2008

After the Second World War, I went to Manchester University to study dentistry and qualified as a dentist in December 1951. I was then commissioned into the Royal Army Dental Corps, serving most of my two years as a Captain in a military hospital in Hong Kong, where I looked after a large number of troops and I was also responsible for the dental care of the soldiers' wives and children.

Having enjoyed looking after children, I decided to spend a couple of years treating them before I settled down in general practice. I joined the School Dental Service in Newport in 1954, working at the clinic in Nine Acres School. It was a happy school and some of the youngsters I cared for then have remained friends for life, including Robert Biggs, George Hibberd and Martin Cave. Miss Packham was Head Mistress, with such dedicated teachers as Irene Fry, Mary Dallimore and Joy Rashley.

Dental disease was at its highest level in the fifties, peaking in 1958. As the School Dentist, my job was to inspect each child annually in the Newport schools, providing treatment where necessary. I would sometimes inspect a school of 300 children without finding one child with a perfect mouth! The average five year old child had five decayed teeth and this situation was not remedied until the sixties, with the help of increasing dental health education and the advent of fluoride toothpaste. I became friendly with the Head Teachers and teachers at the Newport schools, and particularly remember Stan Ward at Carisbrooke Grammar School and Mary Dudgeon at Priory Girls.

At the end of the sixties, we were extremely fortunate in co-operating with Professor Tony Naylor of Guy's Hospital, who was carrying out studies using fluoride toothpaste. In all, we supported four studies over a period of twenty years. My wife, Jean, was the local Administrator who organised the distribution of fluoride toothpaste and toothbrushes to the families of the children taking part - and these numbered over a thousand in each study! The children were given dental health education and inspected each year by the Guy's Team and the immense benefits to these youngsters carried over into their adult lives.

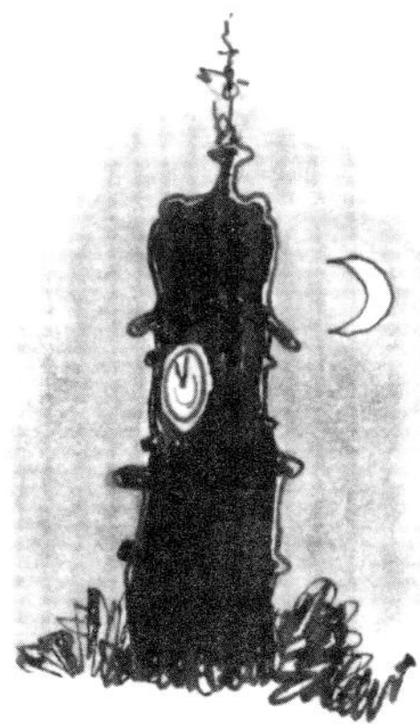

In 1956 I was appointed Dental Officer to Whitecroft Hospital and worked a session each week until the hospital closed nearly forty years later. In the fifties there were nearly 600 patients "under the clock", many of whom were not really mentally ill, but were placed there because they had caused problems at home. Unfortunately, after some years, they became institutionalised and were no longer capable of living independently.

At Whitecroft, I was privileged to work alongside such brilliant doctors as Alex Miller and Eric Laidlaw, who had previously worked at the Royal National Hospital in Ventnor, and were totally dedicated to the welfare of their patients.

Apart from being on call for dental purposes, Jean and I were also on the list of volunteers to help in cases of emergency. On one stormy night, we were called out to help to search for a patient who had gone missing. Some of the patients did tend to wander off the premises but there was a fear that this man might have got lost and could be suffering from the extreme cold. Ivan Linington was in charge of the thirty volunteers and organised groups of us to search in different directions.

Four of us, Chris Orchin, Madeleine Goodman, Jean and I, equipped with a torch and two-way radio, searched one area of the woods along a narrow footpath towards Chillerton. It was pitch dark, pouring with rain and blowing a gale. We searched under the hedges, but without success. After half an hour, we received a message to return as the patient had been found. We gratefully accepted the mug of tea and the biscuits and then Ivan disclosed that the patient had been found hiding in a cupboard on the ward!

I was promoted to Chief Dental Officer for the County Council and at that time I even had a surgery in County Hall where I saw mothers and young children. I also had a great respect for the County Councillors, many of whom had served as high-ranking officers in the forces, such as Rear Admiral Joe Blackham and Brigadier Green. Mollie Christie was in charge of Education, and I also received a great deal of help from Eddie and Gloria Minghella.

The general health of the children was poor in those days. There were outbreaks of poliomyelitis on the Island each year, causing death and disabilities to many children, before the coming of the preventive vaccines.

I used to take lunch with the children in the school hall and sat with their teachers and among them was Noel Britton, who was the peripatetic music teacher. Over lunch one day, he mentioned that they were lacking a double bass in the Youth Orchestra and I volunteered to help as I used to play bass in our school orchestra and also at University. One or two of us older musicians used to help the Youth Orchestra and I played with them for many happy years.

In the 1950s, the Island had few cars and, of course, no large lorries or white vans. I bought my first car from Percy Harwood in 1956 just in time for the Suez Crisis and petrol rationing. At that time I could drive from Wootton to St. Mary's Hospital in the evening without meeting a single car!

The Island at that time was thriving in technology and manufacturing. J.S White's were still building frigates and Decca Radar was developing radar systems on the old Cowes aerodrome. Saunders Roe was building sea planes - including the enormous Princess Flying Boat - but this was never purchased by the government and interest in flying boats diminished following the tragic crash of the Aquila Airways flying boat in November 1957. Saunders Roe went on to develop the Black Knight Rocket and the very first Hovercraft.

I joined the Rotary Club of Newport in 1957 and was

privileged to meet many new friends, including Fred Green the librarian, George Bull the leather merchant, Jim Eldridge the solicitor, Stanley Stevens the butcher Fred Taylor, the accountant, Bill Bennett the optician and Sam Watson and Tom Glenny the auctioneers.

There has been much progress in dental health in the sixty years I have been involved in it. We have gone from being a nation of denture wearers to one where teeth for life is taken for granted. Dentistry itself has changed out of all recognition, with emphasis on preventing disease and maintaining a happy smile.

LIFE AT CHALE SCHOOL 1947 - 1953
by Derek Sprake

Derek Sprake circa 1950

In 2008 we saw signs all over the Island - "Save our Schools" - and my mind was drawn to my earliest memories of school. At the time, the thought of closing schools would have met with an element of joy! I never liked school or, rather, school never liked me.

Perhaps I started with an advantage. My father was the village Carrier and I started working for him from an early age- probably three or four! The day started with a journey from home to Blackgang and back with a stop outside Chale School. Here I saw little children going into this large (or so it seemed then) building but I never saw them coming out! I may have been curious as to what went on inside and, when I was five, I was informed that I too would be entering the village centre of learning.

I can still recall that first day. I was always somewhat taller and larger than others of my age, but I was shown a small bentwood chair with arms similar to which other little children seemed to fit into easily. I didn't - it was too small! It was rather like Goldilocks trying the baby bear's chair! I had to have an 'ordinary' chair to sit on. In fact, I was probably quite proud being given a different chair to everyone else, but in those days I did not like it. I cannot recall having to learn anything that first day but books with letters became a daily event later on, so no doubt they were used to prepare us for the future.

Eventually the torture of not being allowed home was over and presumably someone collected me. I was asked if I had enjoyed school, to which I replied 'No'. But school had not been so bad after all and I had survived. I thought I wouldn't need to go there again but to my utter shock it soon became evident that I had to go again the next day! As it turned out I had to go every day for the next six years- not good news at all! However, I survived Infant School and eventually moved onto Junior School (as it was known then).

Reading was a difficult task at first, although it had its rewards later on. I recall that there was one word I just couldn't read and, as punishment, I had to go back to page one and start again. It took a whole term to finish that book!

We were also forced to eat school food, not like Mum always made, but food which I was told had to be eaten (if not presumably some terrible act would befall me), so I ate it. Food was cooked in the kitchen at the school and was probably of quite a high standard. All was well until we had to eat the obligatory tapioca for sweet. I don't quite know why but we seemed to have it every day - no doubt the government had a ready and cheap supply which had to be used up on children! I have had an aversion to milk puddings of all sorts since then. 'Sit there until it's all gone', was the order and I was even prevented from going outside to play with the others, whom I could only watch enjoying themselves through the window. Torture!

Singing and music was an all important part of our daily curriculum, no doubt because the teachers we had were adept at these arts. It wasn't too bad though and we quite enjoyed these interludes in the otherwise boring daily routine. It led to the occasional concert when parents were invited to attend school and listen to their babies. At Chale School these events always attracted many fathers because the Head Teacher was a buxom widow who, on open days, used her assets to full advantage. Apparently, when she applied for the job (remember this was in the late 1940's) she had dressed soberly but from her first day at school she dressed to impress men, not that we children realised. An unusually low cut dress revealed her bulging assets and the fathers knew that they could enjoy the 'sideshow' at school concerts and appear to be supporting their children!

Those assets were to play an important role in encouraging us to read at a later stage in our education. Friday afternoons were always reserved for 'reading to teacher'. She would sit at her desk and call each boy forward to read to her on a one-to-one basis, placing her right arm around the waist of the unsuspecting child and drawing him tight to her heaving body. This was meant to encourage us to read and although I cannot recall the stories I know that we were all enthusiastic. If you got into the right position you could see down inside the dress and 'they' were visible (remember this was a long time before 'Page 3'). Our aim was to read as slowly as possible- to extend the event- before we returned to our seats. Education came in many forms in those days and I don't think the girls got the same treatment!

Sex education was not part of our lessons. Indeed the word was never used but I do recall a gathering of boys in the lobby, where we hung our coats, because one of the girls was showing them a quick flash of her 'private bits'. She became quite popular and I don't think we were damaged by the experience.

At one time I was given the task of looking after the school goldfish, even taking it home in the holidays. Fridays were the days when the water had to be changed and this was done in the kitchen which was divided from the classroom by a sliding concertina partition. I got quite clever at catching the wriggling fish in a round bowl and providing it with new water. It was quite heavy when full and on one occasion, with wet hands, I dropped the bowl as I was carrying it back to its position on the windowsill at the rear of the classroom. The water spilled over the floor and over everyone sitting nearby but, remarkably, the bowl didn't break and the fish was still encased in his glass prison. He had survived and was quickly provided with more water whilst everyone else got dried. However, I lost my job as goldfish minder!

The arrival of a special pencil sharpener was the subject of much interest. It was a plastic box on a stand with a handle. Pencils were pushed into the box and the handle turned to shave off the wood and reveal the lead, the shavings being collected in the box. It soon became obvious that if you kept pushing the pencil into the sharpener it would soon disappear altogether but this brought about retribution

because pencils were in short supply. This equipment remained screwed to the teacher's desk long after its use was discontinued.

After the War, many things were in short supply and rulers (wooden in those days) were no exception. Stationery was stored in a cupboard at the rear of the classroom and issued sparingly. When our teacher was away, presumably due to illness, a somewhat fierce lady always came to teach us and her method of control was to use a wooden ruler as a mallet, bringing it down with a crash on the desk of the offending pupil. It not only scared the daylights out of us but also usually ended with the ruler disintegrating into splinters. In one week she was guaranteed to dispose of the entire supply of rulers. We soon realised that this was good fun and we deliberately riled her up to 'bring out the ruler', keeping up the trouble until all were broken! What I couldn't understand was why she had to use brand new rulers for her admonishment when there was a ready supply of 'old' rulers which were always ignored.

When our teacher returned she was curious as to where all her rulers had gone and we gladly told her in the hope that the offender would get into trouble - and it had the desired effect! After two such incidents, the rulers were all locked away in a secret place whilst our teacher was away.

It was noted that Chale School always had a regular supply of new books, provided by the 'Seely Library', which were changed regularly. They came in wooden boxes with a sliding panel in front which, when stacked, made a ready bookcase. Other schools were not so lucky and it later transpired that our teacher had become 'friendly' with the librarian who no doubt provided her with all her literary needs and 'extras' on the side. They eventually married and we all benefitted from our ready supply of new books!

The school was a Church of England establishment and the Rector would come into school to teach us 'religion' once a week. We rarely got around to the scriptures but when a church inspector was due to visit we were crammed with God. Long words were used and on one occasion we were asked what the people who go to church were called. The answer was supposed to be 'congregation'. After a long period of silence one boy, who was usually very quiet, put up his hand and said 'Hypocrites, sir', having been told so at home! This event was regularly used in the Rector's sermons in Church after that.

We had a typewriter at home on which I typed my father's invoices etc. Not bad for a seven year old! This skill soon attracted the attention of my teacher because she (or the school) did not have a typewriter so that notices to parents were all handwritten then duplicated on a rubbery system which was the latest invention at the time but long forgotten now. I was asked to type out notices to parents for events such as concerts, jumble sales, etc. (thirty or forty copies). I achieved this with the use of several pieces of carbon paper and typing very slowly, hitting the keys very hard. Even so, my work was sometimes wasted as I had put the carbon paper in the wrong way round! I suppose this made me somewhat special in the eyes of the teacher and I found it soon awarded me celebrity status, which did not find favour with my classmates.

Living two miles from school, we travelled on the Southern Vectis bus, for a fare of 1d (no matter where you got off). To help the conductor, I was made bus prefect and collected all the pennies. This usually produced a long string of tickets from the ticket machine, which I collected and kept at home for many years. Occasionally the bus conductor would issue one ticket for the total value of all the fares, which was a major disappointment. I was also required to report the following day on any bad behaviour on the bus, which I did very conscientiously, presuming that the more incidents I reported would show I was taking my task seriously. 'John stood up before the bus stopped', 'Harry turned round and spoke to Will in the seat behind', 'Jane made a bad smell', were some of the misdemeanours I reported. I was a horrible little boy and my popularity waned rapidly to zero, except with the teacher who praised my enthusiastic attention to the task.

This unpopularity became evident one Christmas. We had a 'postbox', a large cardboard box covered with red crepe paper and a slit in the top. Everyone could put cards to other pupils in the box and they were handed out on the last day of term at the Christmas Party. One year my father had been given a box of unused, but old, cards and I proceeded to write one to every child in the school. As the distribution of cards took place it became clear that my generosity had not been reciprocated, indeed as the last cards were handed out it became clear that I had not received one card. Not one! I believe this had a significant effect on my attitude to others and I realised that I had to make a change. I can't remember how I achieved this but the following year I decided not to send any cards but I received quite a wad from my 'friends'. My reluctance to send Christmas cards to other than special friends still exists to this day.

The risk of children getting lost was not a major issue in the 1950s. The only concern was for their safety from injury, not from strangers. However, one autumn, I did get lost with a friend. He had acquired the Harvest loaf used at the Methodist Church Harvest Festival which was baked by the local baker in the shape of a sheaf of corn. It was only an inch or so thick and basically just crust, so by the time we got it, it was about a week old and was very stale and hard. However, to us it still seemed like a good meal and, for some unknown reason, the two of us decided to take the loaf up to the Hoy Monument on top of St Catherine's Down after school one day and have a feast. This was a journey we had done many times but on the selected day a fog had decided to form over the downs.

We arrived at the monument without trouble and proceeded to try to eat our meal. The loaf was, by now, so hard that we could not even break it with our hands and I think we had to find a stone to hit it to do so. Our teeth also proved unsuitable for such a task and the taste proved that it was inedible. By now we were very hungry, having relinquished our tea at home, and we decided to return to civilisation only to realise that the fog was very thick and we could hardly see in front of our eyes.

My friend knew a different way back to his home and to where we had left our bikes but we decided to stick close to hedges and that would get us home. In fact, this was a very sensible idea which proved exactly the correct method - but it took quite a long time. As we approached our destination, in pitch dark and thick fog, we saw torches being shone and heard voices. Soon we were found and there seemed a relief in the voices of those searching for us. We were not lost but others seemed to think we were. However, that relief soon turned to anger when Dad arrived and I received a clip round the ear and told to get home immediately as 'your mother is worried about you, you stupid boy'. A welcome supper awaited me and I never tried to feast on a Harvest loaf again. So much for the feeding of the five thousand!

Tragedy came in January 1952 when we were about to go on a coach trip to Ryde to see a film. It was to be a rare day off school but at 11am we heard it was cancelled because the King had died. My thoughts were 'B***** the King', why couldn't he have waited until tomorrow to die! The following morning when singing the National Anthem (which we always did in assembly) we had to sing 'God Save the Queen' instead of the King. Was this the end of the world? What was going to happen - and more importantly - when were we going to see the film?

Eventually, after 6 years, life at Chale School came to an end and as I had passed the 'Eleven Plus', I was off to Grammar School in Newport. Every year one 'leaver' received a coveted prize - a copy of Fred Mew's 'Back of the Wight', signed by the great man himself, who happened to be Chairman of the School Managers. I still read on the front page the immortal words - 'To Derek Sprake, for fine work in the school generally and for valued assistance'. As someone said only recently, 'You were only good 'generally' - obviously no good at anything in particular!

POST WAR RYDE by Sandie Owens

Sandie Oakley circa 1950

Growing up in post war Ryde was fun! I lived with my mum and dad in an end of terrace cottage, which was next to land where a house had been bombed. Dad made an allotment using part of the land and built a shed from scrap wood and corrugated iron. When the shed was completed, as a treat because I was only four years old, we had our tea in it.

We had a pocket sized lawn with a border, which was planted every year with salvias, allysum and lobelia (red, white and blue). I was given my own little garden, which was about three feet square, and I spent so much time digging in it with an old spoon that very little managed to grow!

The bomb site was also a magnet for local children as the low walls, re-emerging shrubbery and supply of 'ammo' made it an ideal place to recreate battles or play cowboys and indians. My cousin Mike, almost three years older than me, was my hero as he led the smaller boys in their escapades.

The boys did allow the girls to join in too but they were given menial tasks, such as loading brown paper bags with ground up mortar for use as dust bombs when the battle got under way. Our most important job was to sharpen roof slate into arrow heads, which were then fastened into the ends of split cane with string, for use as pretty lethal arrows. I'm amazed no one was seriously hurt. What would the health and safety gurus have to say about that today?

We also built dens from whatever we could find and hollowed out hedges for the same purpose. In these dens we ate our picnic lunches, stored treasures in old biscuit tins and created imaginary scenarios that were acted out with great enthusiasm.

I never realised how little my parents had, as they were always so positive and made the best of everything. Looking back, I can remember Friday nights when my dad would bring home his pay and work out the week's bills to see if he could afford to catch the bus to Wootton or whether he would have to leave an hour early to walk to work the next week.

We had an outside loo and a galvanised bath The bath was brought in from outside, put in front of the fire and filled using buckets of hot water. When not in use, the bath hung on the wall of the outside loo and dad grew a pretty Dorothy Perkins climbing rose on an arbour in front of it so that it was not in view.

All of the children in the neighbourhood used to call at our house - especially when mum had been baking. During our 'battles' on the bomb site, any injured parties were taken to our kitchen, lifted up onto the draining board and their wounds cleaned and bandaged. Then they were sent on their way to fight another day.

I am so glad that technology had not caught up with us in the 1940s as the games and stories we told each other made us use our imaginations to the full. We were healthy and happy - if a little dirty at times. The food we ate was wholesome and not processed to infinity and we learned to be resourceful, as we had to 'make do' most of the time. Tips from older relatives have stayed with me to this day, such as taking a pride in doing a job well. My grandfather used to say 'if a job's worth doing, it's worth doing well', and he wasn't wrong!

LIFE IN SHORWELL DURING THE WAR
by Peggy Thompson

Peggy Thompson 1931

My sister and I were born in the village of Wroxall. We moved, as very young children, to Chillerton for, I think, about two years, then to Shorwell where we spent all of our growing up years. They were happy years, spent in a loving home.

During those years the war came and the peacefulness of our village was somewhat shattered. Houses were requisitioned (the largest being Northcourt) and these houses stationed the troops. The first to arrive was the Second Batallion of the Royal Fusiliers, a London company with cockney accents, so different to our own.

LIFE AT HOME

Mother had a small tea room, but with the arrival of the troops, this rapidly turned into a canteen and a home from home. My parents made the soldiers very welcome and our home was full. My mother said that she hoped someone would look after her son as she tried to do for the boys stationed here. They called her 'Ma' and her hospitality did not stay just with the men as we often had a wife staying with us for good measure. We even had the Bren gun carriers, which were like small tanks, parked outside. The village boys were most impressed.

The soldiers were allowed in most rooms in the house but not the front room or upstairs. One soldier I shall always remember was the one who became very famous and his name was Eric Morley. He and his wife were responsible for the Miss World programmes on the television in later years. Chairs were always full so he sat in the kitchen on an oil drum, which was our coal bin. I remember, to our fascination, he used to put vinegar on his eggs.

We, as a family, had an indoor air raid shelter. This was a very large table type which filled one of our rooms, originally the dining room, but long taken over by the troops. My sister, Sylvia, and I used to get in under the mattress and listen in on conversations. One lady who was a constant amusement to us was a retired school teacher who lived a little way up the road. Every time there was an air raid warning red, down she'd come to sit under our stairs. She always wore what was called a siren suit, the same sort as Winston Churchill wore, and she brought the deeds of her house and anything important to her in a suitcase. She was a very tall, forbidding sort of lady and married to the air raid warden, who spent his time in the air raid post which was in the village hall.

The warden had quite a broad accent and when the raid was over he would ring my mother and say 'Air raid warning green and no casualties.' He would arrive on his bike and come to visit his wife under the stairs. My sister and I would wait with handkerchiefs stuffed in our mouths to stop us laughing aloud! She had rather a loud, deep voice which seemed very funny to us and would say 'Kiss me William', which was quite out of character, or so we thought. Later on, when the air raids were not quite so frequent, I was detailed to go to sleep in her house right under the thatch, which I thought was rather dangerous.

The boys who manned the field telephones found that they could ring my mother on our phone and they would order sandwiches, nearly always egg, when they were on guard half way up Shorwell Shute or down by the church on guard duty. There were no plastic boxes or bags in those days, so brown paper bags were the order of the day. Bearing in mind we had no lights or torches, when the order came for two egg sandwiches, off I'd go up the Shute, brown bags in hand. Out of the darkness came the cry, 'Halt who goes there?' 'Pass Peggy, be recognised'. Most nights I was up and down the Shute and up and down the main road on the same errand.

Peggy 1942

AIR RAIDS

My father took charge of the Demolition Squad and was stationed in Freshwater. He found himself there most nights as there was usually an air raid.

One night in an air raid, when the planes had passed over, we opened the front door and everywhere, including the front steps, was covered in incendiary bombs - it was as if the stars had dropped and the village was alight. One house, at the bottom of the Shute, was on fire. No one was hurt in this raid but the thatched house was gutted. One amusing thing out of all this was the fact that our father had pulled his onions and laid them out to dry and those 'Jerries' had burnt them all, which dad did not find amusing - he was really angry.

Another time, a bomb fell in the Council yard beside

our home - quite a bang. However, our house had walls three feet thick and not a pane of glass was broken. There is another house built in that space now. We didn't get away without some disaster though as a house in Yafford had a direct hit and people were killed.

In 1943 my elder sister, her daughter and unborn child were killed in an air raid in Shanklin, as she was visiting her in-laws when it happened. The gas works were hit and seven firemen from London who were sent down to have a break from the fierce bombing lost their lives as well.

Once, early in the war, it was announced that in the case of gas being used, the warden would ride through the village on his bike, with a football rattle. One sunny afternoon in August, in our garden, I was up in the sky as high as I could get on our swing when, down the road, came the warden with his rattle having a practise! I jumped, not waiting for the swing to come down and I landed up to my armpits in my father's pig manure heap! My poor mother had to hose me down - and all for a gas attack practise!!

DOING OUR BIT

Speaking of pigs, we had two in our sty - we couldn't just have one. It had to be registered with the local police who came round to check the pig book to make sure we were not cheating with more than two or less than two. When my father had to send the pigs for slaughter, one went into the food chain for the Ministry of Food and we could keep the other. When it came back, my sister and I were sent round the village with parcels of meat for those who had no pigs to slaughter, so everyone had some fresh pork.

As most men of the village were called up, my sister and I used to go to the farms, get the cattle in from the fields and help in the milking parlours. I also remember having to scrub their feet, poor things. They used to get such hard feet from all the mud that we had to treat them using a substance called Stockholm Tar. It was real messy stuff but I think it used to form a protective covering.

We also took our money to school for savings stamps to help the war effort and knitted for victory. In those days, I could turn the heel of a sock- but not now.

SOCIAL LIFE

We used to have concerts in the village hall and back then it didn't matter how many we got into the place - the more the merrier. There was no other entertainment at the time so our efforts were eagerly awaited.

The whist drives were quite something. My sister was really good at it - but not me. I went along, much to everyone's utter disbelief - they groaned when I went in. 'Oh no' could be heard around the hall and I spoiled quite a few games for them but I was blissfully unaware of the havoc I caused.

My sister and her friend were what they called the 'Spitfire Band'. They entertained the children with song and dance in a shed at the top of our garden. It cost a halfpenny to get in and refreshments were supplied by mum. Of course the whole amount gained was only six pence but our rector,

who was a truly lovely man, would take it with grateful thanks. We also had to collect conkers and take them in sacks to the rectory - something to do with oil but I cannot remember what it was used for.

On Sundays we had a marching band with bugles and drums that led the boys on Church parade. They were the Church of England lads as Catholics were taken into Newport in an army truck. The Methodists joined our family and walked to the Chapel up in the village and more often than not they were invited to stay to lunch.

The village was also home to evacuees. We always had two, perhaps more, and they were always up to something. The nearby beach was an attraction but strictly out of bounds. This didn't stop them from climbing the cliffs from above and coming home with seagulls eggs which my mother cooked for them, albeit they were a bit fishy! After these escapades they very rarely had a pair of shorts that weren't ripped to pieces!

TOWARDS THE END OF THE WAR AND AFTERWARD

All of our childhood spent in Shorwell was a happy one. In the wartime, everyone was there for each other and if there were things to share we did just that. As a village we picked ourselves up, dusted ourselves down and got on with things.

When I was growing up there were many men in the village with a very pronounced Isle of Wight dialect. One such, or rather more than one, worked for dad and when they came to the door to request something it was either I or my sister who answered and we could not understand half of what they were saying!

During the war my father had a revolver which was kept in readiness for any eventuality. After the war he built a wall in the garden, wrapped the thing in old silk and built it into the wall. Years afterwards, when the next owner of our house knocked down the wall he found it and the police were at mum's door - apparently the thing was in perfect condition and could be fired at any time!

Towards the end of the war when the soldiers were nearly all gone, the 'canteen' was shut and my mother became the village postmistress, which lasted quite a number of years. During a break in my nursing career I took on the twice daily village post round. I had to go in all weathers rain, snow or sun on a bike with a large basket on the front. It was a very long round, but it kept me fit!

LIFE IN THE WOMEN'S LAND ARMY
by Sybil Groves (nee Burford)

Sybil Burford 1942

I joined the Women's Land Army in 1942 when I was 17. I wanted to join the WRAF but my mother said a firm 'No' to that idea. I married in 1943 and carried on living at home at Heath Farm, Colwell, as my husband was in the army and stationed in Iceland. His leave was only seven days each year including travelling time so we saw very little of each other. Our plan was to save up as much money as we could so that we could set up our home together on the Island after the war.

Throughout the war I and 23 other girls were based at Dunsbury Farm in Brook. Mr Walmsley was the farmer, Mr Thompson the foreman and Percy Cotton the bailiff. It was a large farm and ran all the way from the downs to the coast and along to Compton.

The Land Army girls were mainly from the West Wight - Brighstone, Brook, Calbourne, Freshwater and Hulverstone - with just two girls coming over from Shanklin. They lodged locally during the week. When we joined the land army, we were provided with a very smart uniform that we wore at the weekend when we went out - although most of the time we were in our dungarees (our dismals) with a shirt in the summer and a jumper in the winter.

Every morning, two of us met at Freshwater Station at 6.30am and cycled over to Brook for a 7.00am start. I remember the soldiers on the guns at Tapnell shouting out to us as we went by every morning and evening.

The work included following behind a tractor and planting potatoes. We started that task in February, worked through till noon and then stopped for a one hour lunch break when we usually had sandwiches. I remember mine being cheese and onion most of the time. If it was cold, we used to go down to Hanover Stores in Brook for a nice hot cup of Horlicks. We finished at 5.00pm in the winter. In the summer, we worked until we had

finished what we were doing. On a really good week I could earn £2. Those weeks usually included some piece rate work. I remember cutting and trimming cabbages for 6d (2p) a bag. All our produce went to Fred Trim's, the wholesaler, who had premises in Pyle Street in Newport.

There were no animals at Dunsbury so sometimes we had no work to do there and went elsewhere. I remember going down to Appleford for spud picking on the back of a trailer and we sang all the way there and all the way back.

We also went to Freshwater Fruit Farm in Wilmingham Lane to plant tomatoes in the greenhouses there. Freshwater Fruit Farm had been bombed before I went there and I saw it happen. It was on my Thursday afternoon off and my friend and I were out for a walk over Afton Down when the planes came over. We thought the pilots had seen us and were bombing us. I was petrified as they came in over our heads and dropped their bombs on the greenhouses below us. As I was working at 'Orchards' (I worked there when I left school when I was 15, just after the war started) in Freshwater Bay at the time it must have been in 1940 or 1941.

We worked Monday to Friday and had the weekends off. Saturday highlights included a visit to the Regent Cinema in Freshwater where Somerfield is now. Sometimes I would cycle over to Carisbrooke and stay with my mother-in-law and we walked down to Newport to the pictures. There were no buses.

I'm not sure what would have happened if I had joined the WRAF. I do know that I had a good time working with a terrific team of girls and was probably the fittest I've ever been!

**Sybil Burford
Ethel Cotton and
Dorothy Baxter 1942**

MY EARLIEST MEMORIES OF FRESHWATER FRUIT FARM by John Craddock.

John Craddock circa 1955

As a child I lived at Tollgate Cottages, Wilmingham Lane, Freshwater and my mum was friends with Mrs Pocock who lived at Freshwater Fruit Farm. Her husband was the manager there and they grew tomatoes in the greenhouses in the summer, followed by chrysanthemums for cutting around the Christmas period when there was a big demand for flowers. Freesias were also grown in one of the greenhouses and they always smelt wonderfully. Whenever I smell freesias now, half a century or more later, I still get the image in my head of that greenhouse. Outside crops included potatoes, runner beans and I think, on occasions, broad beans. I'm sure there were other crops but I can't remember any.

Mr and Mrs Pocock had a son called Martin, who was a year older than me. No other children lived nearby, so we were good friends and I used to like going to play at Martin's house because there was so much to do and lots of space. Martin's grandparents owned Barnsfield Farm, just a mile down the road, so it was always fun to go there - except that I remember there was a goose that

would attack me! Maybe it was a gander, either way I tried not to go too close if I saw it before it saw me!

In those days (early to mid 1950's) about six full time employees worked at Freshwater Fruit Farm and in the summer quite a number of part time employees as well. I can also remember my mum picking runner beans there when I was quite small.

There were five green houses that were 120'x30', one a little smaller and one they called "Big 'Ouse", this was a double span and so was probably 120'x 60'. So there was close to two thirds of an acre in total, which is not much by today's standards but was a lot in those days. The glass panes were only 12 inches wide and were curved inward at the top and downward at the bottom. This had the effect of making rain water flow down the middle of the glass and away from the wooden glazing bars.

I can just remember seeing sets of narrow gauge railway tracks piled up and little metal trucks. These were moved into the green houses to transport bulky items in or out. There was also a steam sterilizer which would have run on these rails. The remains of the sterilizer is still there but it's rusting slowly away under some trees and the remains of the wheels would show the gauge of the tracks. This device can be seen on an aerial photo taken in 1959, it shows up quite well, as it's white, covered we assume with the wonder insulator of the day - asbestos!

The green houses were heated with coke, which is coal but with the gas taken out. The coke came from the local gasworks at Yarmouth. The boilers were below ground level, with a pitched roof starting at ground level. They had to be stoked up frequently in cold weather and during the night too. I can remember watching Martin's dad climbing down the ladder and shovelling the coke onto the furnace and raking

Freshwater Fruit Farm circa 1959

through the clinker. The worst part about it was the awful sulphur fumes, which really hurt the chest when breathed in and there was no way to avoid it. It was not a pleasant job for whoever had to do it and it must have been especially hard to leave a warm bed in the middle of the night to get up, trudge through the snow (we used to get snow in those days), or frost and cough your lungs out in several dingy stokeholes. What a good idea oil and thermostats were!

There was a well and a water tower and we sometimes went to watch the old engine pumping water up into the 2000 gallon tank about 25 feet above, this water was then gravity fed when needed for the crops in the greenhouses.

The rain water was all collected from the greenhouse roofs and went via a concrete channel into a reservoir. There were a lot of great crested newts in this reservoir and Martin and I used to sometimes catch some of them - we always returned them unharmed of course. The reservoir was filled in around 1969 and unfortunately this colony of great crested newts was destroyed. When we moved here in 1972, I had the reservoir dug out again and we had some newts back within a week or two, however the only species since have been the smooth newt (common newt) and the palmate newt. I have been trying, without success so far, to get great crested newts established again but due to their scarcity have been unable to hear of any that need relocating - such a shame.

The house was built in 1934 and had its own gas generating plant, although I'm not sure how it worked. There was a shed with a device, whatever it was, inside and a tall iron construction with a big, round concrete block, attached to steel wires going to the top with pulleys. Somehow the weight of the round concrete block must have provided pressure for the gas to be used in the house. That's all gone but in our loft there are still some of the pipes that took the gas and also a fitting or two on a couple of walls. I can also just remember the wooden shutters that were around the windows, I suppose these were for use during the war.

Both my mum and Martin's mum were nervous of lightning (we used to get more of that years ago as well). If there was a storm brewing, or thunder rumbling around, my mum and I would cycle down here as quick as we could and shelter with Mrs Pocock and Martin under the stairs, the exact spot is about 8 feet from where I'm typing this account.

The wooden shed, which must have been built at the same time as the greenhouses, was used as a packing shed and still stands today. Martin and I must have spent hours cycling round and round it on our bikes.

There were a lot of Cuppressus macrocarpa trees used as a windbreak planted around the place to protect the greenhouses from the south and east winds. These get top heavy fairly quickly and even in those days some used to blow over. They seemed huge to us as kids and we used to climb them quite a lot. They were also used as firewood and, when cut, the wood has a characteristic smell of disinfectant. When I smell that nowadays it reminds me of the trees we used to climb. There are still a couple of these trees left but they are starting to lean a bit now and will not last much longer.

The two bomb craters that Mrs. Sybil Groves mentions in her "Life in the Women's Land Army" account held great fascination for us as boys and we often went to look at them. They are still in evidence in 2009!

I seem to have had a long association with Freshwater Fruit Farm. I played here from probably about the age of a toddler. I worked here in my summer holidays and at weekends in 1962 when I was 13. Then again about five months after I left school in 1965, I worked here for about eight months. Then my wife Brenda and I moved back from Worcestershire to live here in 1972 and we've been here ever since. I hadn't planned to work here after I left school, it was just by chance and it was an even stranger set of events that led to us moving back here in 1972 - but that's another story.

REFLECTIONS OF FARMING PRIOR TO 1970
by Malcolm Dyer

Malcom Dyer 2008

Everything changes and farming on the Isle of Wight is no exception. I left school early in the 1950s and attended the Agriculture Course at the West Wight Secondary Modern School (Pre Ag it was called), where about six hours of our school week was taken up in agriculture and horticulture on the school farm and gardens.

Most farms were much smaller than today and were, to a large extent, family mixed farms, having a herd of milking cows (40 was a big herd then), some beef cattle, probably several sows and sties of pigs. Some farms had flocks of sheep and nearly all would have some poultry laying hens and chickens for the Christmas trade. Only a few people seemed able to afford the few turkeys that were about.

A lot of farms, even quite small ones, grew several fields of corn and most were still being harvested in sheaves with binders. The ricks were threshed by the threshing machine that went from farm to farm in the winter months. Combines were very small to start with, only cutting 4-5 ft at a time, whilst some were pulled by tractor with another engine powering the combine.

My memories of those days tell me that all the food that could be produced was needed. During the mid 1950s to 1960s most farmers were trying to produce more, either by keeping more stock, using more fertilisers or buying or renting extra land. More machinery of every description was being purchased and the good, faithful carthorse was disappearing from farms in big numbers.

There were always some large, arable and mixed farms and the Island prided itself on several large vegetable growers. The Newchurch area, even then, was famous for its glasshouses and nurserymen. Tomatoes and potatoes were seasonal and early, along with strawberries and other soft fruit. After tomatoes had finished, most filled their greenhouses with crysanthemums that made good money in Covent Garden, London, for the winter and Christmas trade. They were taken daily by train from Newport Railway Station.

They were good days (proof that I'm getting older?). The Young Farmers Clubs were strong, with Newport, Ryde, Shanklin and the Agricultural Pre Ag Courses being the fourth club. We had visits to farms, nurseries, creameries, mills, shows and an annual competition within the Isle of Wight Ploughing Match. Classes were in stock judging, pig judging, digging, poultry plucking, poultry dressing, thatching, patching (hessian sacks) and public speaking, etc. There was always plenty to do.

pig judging

I do remember that at Christmas each year all the work that could be done beforehand, was done, and that only left the milking and feeding of farm animals for Christmas Day and Boxing Day, so that workers could relax and have a well earned rest. May all who work on our farms have a good relaxation every Christmas!

MY LIFE IN THE WILDERNESS
by Alan S.Philpott

Alan Philpott circa 1957

We had lived in lovely, civilized Brading for several years when my parents sold our chocolate box cottage in West Street and moved half a mile along the road to Yarbridge. My grandparents had bought what seemed to me as a small child, a massive rambling ruin called Nutbourne. The idea was for my Mum and Dad to renovate it using the proceeds of the sale of our cottage. When finished, my grandparents would move down from Essex and we would all live there happily ever after, running the place as a guest house with holiday cottages in the old stables that were in the garden.

Things have a funny way of not working out quite as planned. I think it was late in 1954 and my parents had spent all their money on the holiday project when a squabble with Grandma and Grandad resulted in us moving out. We ended up renting an old farm cottage somewhere out in a 'wilderness' that my dad said was Wootton Common.

It cannot be denied that Keepers Cottage was picturesque, with a long sloping roof on one side that came down as far as the ground floor windows. The garden was a kid's dream with plenty of space to play and being surrounded by fields, so I could make as much noise as I liked.

I enrolled in Havenstreet Primary School, a

threequarters of a mile walk down the farm track plus a bus ride from home. I soon found I had two new friends who lived on a farm that was even deeper into the 'wilderness' than our cottage.

My Dad had managed to save one luxury, an old Ford V8 car that was practically worthless because it drank so much expensive petrol. On special occasions he would treat me and my new pals to a lift down the lane to the school bus stop, but this was only if the trip could be combined with an essential journey because of the cost of the fuel.

I was 8 years old, but still unable to grasp the mysteries of how to read. At Brading school I had found the 'Beacon' reading books such boring things that there was no incentive to really try and I couldn't get past the infants book three. Havenstreet Primary opened a new door to me. "What reading book are you on?" asked Mr Farthing, a tall friendly sounding man who was my new teacher. This was a dream come true. I had longed to look at the grown up stories in book six, so with no thought that I might later be tested on it, I squeaked out "Book six". I never did get found out and in no time at all I was reading as well as the rest of the children in the school. Maybe there is a lesson for teachers to learn from this... of course it was a long time ago, so perhaps they have. I wonder?

Life in the cottage was certainly different to what we

had been used to. At our cottage in Brading, the toilet was at the end of the garden, but here it was right by the back door. To me that was a luxury, but to Dad it was bad news as there was no drainage system connected to it. The WC was an ancient chemical affair with a large bucket under the seat. Every few days Dad had the 'pleasant' task of digging a hole in some 'convenient' part of the garden where he would empty the horrible thing and then put the turf back on top! After we had been there a few weeks, finding a fresh place to dig became increasingly difficult. Deciding there had to be a better way of dealing with this problem, he chose a remote corner of the garden and dug a massive hole. I will leave the rest to your imagination but suffice to say that my pals and I never played anywhere near it! I wonder if the people who have lived there since ever wonder why their garden is so fertile!

In the mid 1950s there were still lots of houses on the island that did not have mains electricity. Most that were not connected to the mains had generators but Keepers Cottage was an exception to this. Luckily, we were no strangers to oil lamps and candles as that was all we had during the four years we had lived on a boat. Life ashore had softened us though, so before long Dad was searching for an affordable generating set. Family friends Phyllis and Don came to the rescue. They owned a huge World War 2 landing craft which they had converted into a floating hotel. From somewhere deep in the bilges of this ship, Don had removed the ship's original generator and had been planning to sell it at Newport market. It now had a new home in our shed!

Things were now looking up and we settled into the country life quite well. A few chickens and a cockerel were added to our family which also included Blackie the cat, who for some reason my Dad called Black Pooper! Perhaps Blackie had his own pet names for us when he went digging in the garden as cats do!

I can't remember the cockerel's name, but whatever it was, he was a miserable devil. He hated everybody and would attack anyone who got close to him. Maybe he was only protecting his harem of hens that were doing a good job keeping us supplied with eggs but after he savaged the postman it was decided he would have to go. Dad asked the farmer about the correct way to dispatch a chicken. I am not sure if it was because he didn't like the 'hands on' method he was told about, or if it was that our bird was impossible to catch, but Dad decided on what he considered a more humane method - he would shoot it.

No, he didn't have a shotgun, but he did still have a wartime relic in the form of a .455 Webley service revolver. I can confirm that headless chickens do run around the garden! Whatever his name was, the cockerel had the last laugh on us though. Far from a delicious treat for Sunday dinner (it was dinner in those days, not lunch!), we were all too miserable about the execution to enjoy it. On top of that, he was as tough as the proverbial old boots. And the gun - I think it ended up somewhere at the bottom of the Solent!

Don's generator not only gave us light, it also gave us entertainment. As a small kid I had always enjoyed listening to the 'wireless'. My favourite programme was 'Journey into Space', although I was constantly being reminded by my wiser elders that it was all a lot of nonsense and that men would never travel into space, let alone land on the moon! You can be sure I reminded them of that just 15 years later when Neil Armstrong sent back his "The Eagle has landed" message from the Moon. With no television, the wireless was our major source of modern entertainment and as a special treat I would be allowed to stay up to listen to 'The Huggets' which was broadcast at 8.30pm.

All this cheer did come at some cost as the generator had to be started by hand. As it got to dusk, Dad would disappear out to the shed and the light would soon come on. Many times it would soon go off again. This usually happened after Dad had got back indoors and settled down with his slippers on, a cup of tea and a pipe of revolting tobacco mixture he made from some cheap herbal stuff and a pinch of the real thing! With Dad just ready for a snooze and Walter Gabriel of 'The Archers' halfway through some broadcasting gem, the lights would suddenly go dim, then bright, then dim again and then off. This was the classic symptoms of dirt in the carburettor and the cue for Dad to teach me some new words for my vocabulary! With dad back in the shed, Mum and I would watch the lights glimmer for a second or two every time Dad tried to restart the ****** thing (as he called it). Eventually

the lights would come on properly and Dad would get back just in time to hear the music at the end of 'The Archers'.

The much cursed generator did bring another benefit other than the unreliable supply of electricity. It started on petrol and was then switched over to run on a tractor fuel called TVO, which was similar to paraffin and much cheaper than petrol. This gave Dad the idea that he could do the same with his old Ford! As this was not at all legal, it became my job to go down to the farm and buy fuel "for the generator" so as not to raise any suspicions. Mr Renton, the farmer, must have wondered what sort of lights we had to burn the amount of TVO our little power plant was using!

Winter in the wilderness saw me become a young vandal! Walking down the lane after school one particularly cold day, the Renton boys and I came across a new looking motorbike parked to one side of the track. I suppose the vandals of today would have wrecked it - but I had a much better idea. A big puddle of muddy water nearby was frozen solid and, with a great deal of effort, we managed to prize it from the ground. Then with great delight we lifted it onto the saddle of the gleaming motorcycle! What a lovely present it would be for the owner on his return and we happily skipped on our way home - a good job, well done!

When I got indoors, horror of horrors, there was my favourite big cousin, Bernard, a bit of a hero to me because he was a member of a skiffle group. "Hello little stinger" he said, "I was going to bring my new motorbike down to show you but the lane was so bumpy and muddy I didn't want to get it dirty!" Luckily, Bernard is now a good Christian gentleman, so when I confessed my youthful misdemeanour to him a couple of years ago he didn't go straight out and smear mud all over the seats of my car!

A couple of Gypsy families lived in their caravans in a

clearing in the woods near Havenstreet and their children went to the village school. One day I was told that Grandma was coming over to meet me on the bus from school and then coming to see our little house. On the bus I whispered to Grandma to look out for the Gypsy caravans as I thought she would be interested. When I pointed them out she loudly asked in her cockney voice, "Is that where those Didicoys live?" I cringed as the bus ground to a halt to let the Gypsy children off. Next day one of them came over to me and said "We're not Didicoys, we are Gypsies!" and promptly punched me on the nose! I still don't know the exact difference and I am not asking! And the reason Grandma was visiting? It turned out that the rift with my grandparents had more or less been healed and we would go back to live with them.

Despite the hardships of being desperately poor I had a great life during our time at Keepers Cottage. My arms must have grown several inches longer with all the cans of TVO I carried from the farm for our 'generator' but at least Dad could afford to drive us around in the car.

The opportunity to explore seemingly endless acres of farmland with the other boys was akin to being somewhere out on the prairie, a wonderful freedom not enjoyed by many of today's kids. I even learned how to - or should I say how not to - ride a cow to the milking shed and how to fix those sucker things of the milking machine to her udders. No, they didn't use a three legged stool and do it by hand, but we did get fresh milk every day and it was always still warm. After six months, our life on Wootton Common was coming to an end and ... well that's another story.

INDEPENDENT ARTS

Therapeutic Art Projects in the Community

Charity No: 297474 Company limited by guarantee No: 2147908

Become a Friend of Independent Arts

Anyone who gives a donation of £10 or more will become a Friend of Independent Arts for one year.

You will receive newsletters giving an update on projects and invitations to our events. There will also be some discounts available.

You will have the satisfaction of knowing that you are helping people with special needs on the Isle of Wight.

Make your donation go further through Gift Aid, by filling in the form on the reverse page.

I would like to become a Friend of Independent Arts

Name..

Address...

....

Tel No: ....

Email: ....

Thank you. There is a Standing Order form on the reverse page if you would like to donate regularly.

Standing Order Mandate

Independent Arts Charity Number 297474 Company limited by guarantee No: 2147908

Bank Sort Code	
Bank Address	
Bank Address	
Bank Address	
Your Account Name	
Your Account Number	

To ______________________________ (Your bank)

Please set up the following STANDING ORDER and debit my/our account accordingly. Pay: Independent Arts, Shide Road, Newport, Isle of Wight, PO30 1HR

Account Number 00006233 Sort Code 40-52-40

The sum of £...........on the first day of ....(month) yearly, commencing ....(year) until further notice .

Your signature .... Date............

Please post this form to: Independent Arts, Shide Road, Newport, Isle of Wight, PO30 1HR

Gift Aid

I am a UK taxpayer and qualify for Gift Aid* and I want Independent Arts to claim tax back on all donations I make in the future, until I notify Independent Arts otherwise.

Signature.. Date.......................

*To qualify for Gift Aid, what you pay in income tax or capital gains tax must at least equal the amount we will reclaim in the tax year. It is vital that you let us know if this changes, or if you change address.

THANK YOU FOR YOUR SUPPORT